EASY CLASSIC

DUETS 2

8 EXCITING ARRANGEMENTS

BY GLENDA AUSTIN, ERIC BAUMGARTNER,
MELODY BOBER, AND CAROLYN MILLER

ISBN 978-1-70515-822-7

WILLIS MUSIC

EXCLUSIVELY DISTRIBUTED BY

HAL•LEONARD®

© 2022 by The Willis Music Co.
International Copyright Secured All Rights Reserved

Visit Hal Leonard Online at
www.halleonard.com

Contact us:
Hal Leonard
7777 West Bluemound Road
Milwaukee, WI 53213
Email: info@halleonard.com

In Europe, contact:
Hal Leonard Europe Limited
42 Wigmore Street
Marylebone, London, W1U 2RN
Email: info@halleonardeurope.com

In Australia, contact:
Hal Leonard Australia Pty. Ltd.
4 Lentara Court
Cheltenham, Victoria, 3192 Australia
Email: info@halleonard.com.au

ABOUT THE COMPOSERS

The German composer **Johann Sebastian BACH** needs no introduction and is revered by musicians for his complex and contrapuntal compositions. In his day (1685-1750) he was much more famous as a virtuosic organist. He is also infamous for having 20 children.

Léo DELIBES was a French ballet and opera composer who lived from 1836 to 1891. The Flower Duet is from the opera "Lakmé," and its dazzling melody has been used in popular culture for numerous films and ads. Lakmé is French for Lakschmi, the Hindu goddess of wealth.

Johann PACHELBEL was a German composer who lived from 1653 to 1706 and "Canon in D" is his most famous work. The piece was rediscovered in 1919, and you will recognize it from wedding preludes and other special occasions, where it is often arranged for piano, organ, or string quartet. It was originally written for three violins and basso continuo.

Giacomo PUCCINI was an Italian opera composer who lived from 1858 to 1924. His operas are romantic and full of lingering melodies. "O mio babbino caro" is sung by a daughter to her father telling him to give the boy she loves another chance.

Russian composer and virtuoso pianist **Sergei RACHMANINOFF** (1873-1943) is known for his poignant and incredibly demanding piano works. The vocalise in this collection is his most remembered and was originally written for piano and soprano. Because of the Russian revolution of 1917, Rachmaninoff emigrated to the United States with his family in 1918.

Gioachino ROSSINI was an Italian opera composer who lived from 1792 to 1868. The melodies from the overture to the Guillaume Tell grand opera is often associated with horseback riding, likely because it was the theme music for the tv series "The Lone Ranger!" Interestingly, Rossini retired from composing while still in his 30s.

Chevalier de SAINT-GEORGES is known as the first classical composer of African ancestry. He was born Joseph Bologne in 1745 in the Caribbean archipelago of Guadeloupe. His father was a wealthy plantation owner and his mother an enslaved person. After moving to France, he was initially better known to the public as a quick, skillful fencer, taking part in several championships. Crowds were amazed when they saw him playing the violin in an orchestra. He composed several violin concerti, chamber music, and symphonies before he died at age 53.

Clara SCHUMANN, born in 1819, was a child prodigy. Today she is regarded as the preeminent pianist of her time. She started touring at age 9 and performed internationally throughout her life, with over 1300 concert performances! Her future husband Robert witnessed one of these performances, fell in love with both her and music, and stopped his law studies to himself study music. Schumann loved to compose, especially before her hectic concert schedule and family duties took precedence. Her piano trio was written for piano, violin, and cello and is frequently cited as one of her masterpieces. She died in 1896.

CONTENTS

4 William Tell Overture
GIOACHINO ROSSINI

10 O mio babbino caro
GIACOMO PUCCINI

14 Symphonie Concertante No. 1
CHEVALIER DE SAINT-GEORGES

20 Flower Duet
LÉO DELIBES

24 Jesu, Joy of Man's Desiring
JOHANN SEBASTIAN BACH

30 Canon in D
JOHANN PACHELBEL

36 Vocalise
SERGEI RACHMANINOFF

40 Piano Trio in G Minor
CLARA SCHUMANN

William Tell Overture

SECONDO

Gioachino Rossini
1792–1868
Arranged by Glenda Austin

Not too fast, but with precision

William Tell Overture

PRIMO

Gioachino Rossini
1792–1868
Arranged by Glenda Austin

Not too fast, but with precision

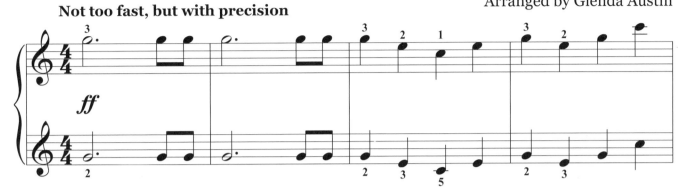

SECONDO

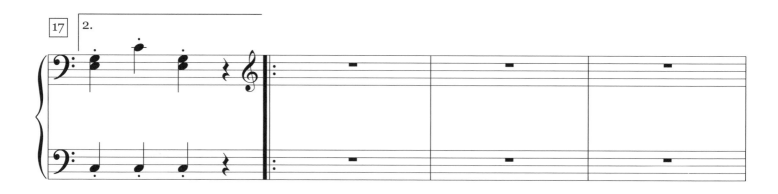

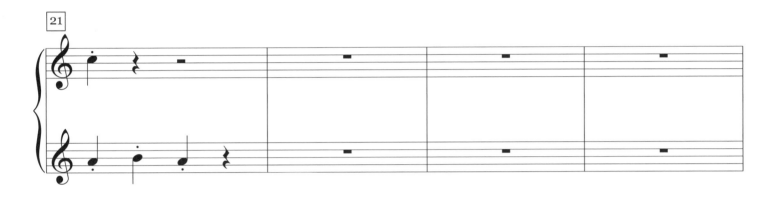

SECONDO

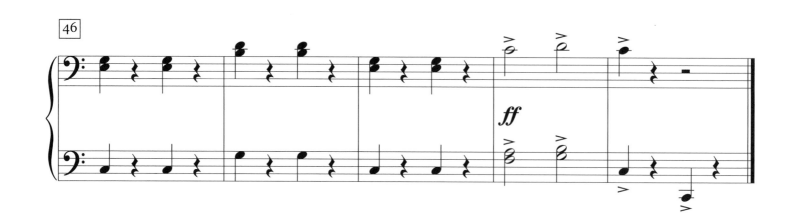

PRIMO

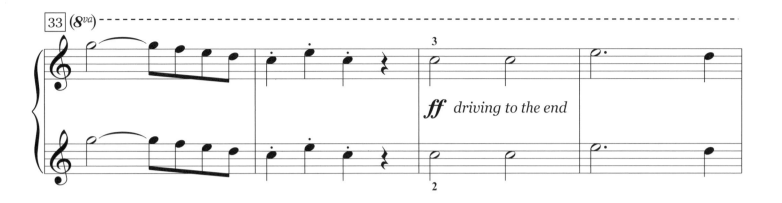

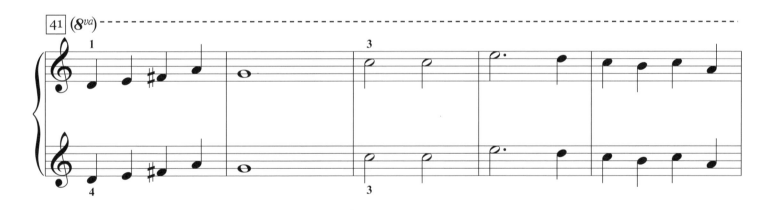

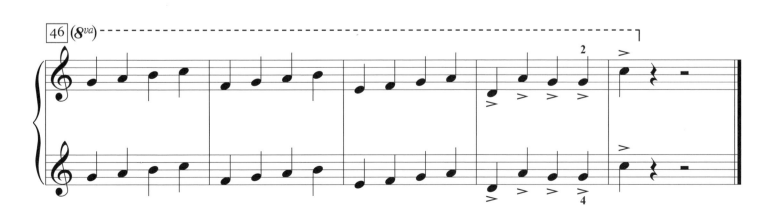

O mio babbino caro

from *Gianni Schicchi*

SECONDO

Giacomo Puccini
1858–1924
Arranged by Carolyn Miller

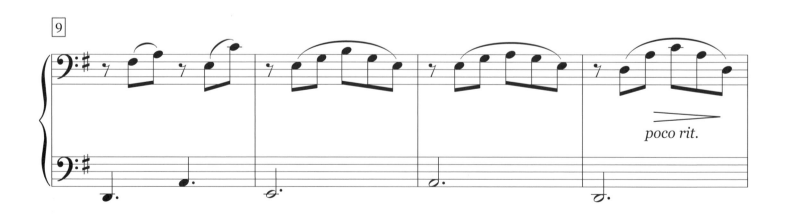

O mio babbino caro

from *Gianni Schicchi*

PRIMO

Giacomo Puccini
1858–1924
Arranged by Carolyn Miller

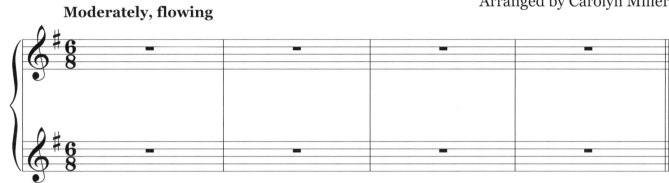

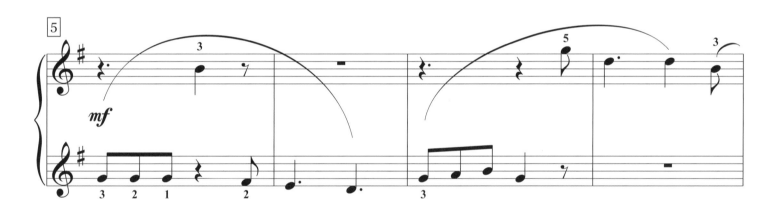

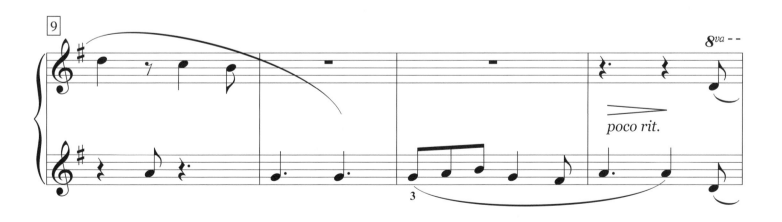

SECONDO

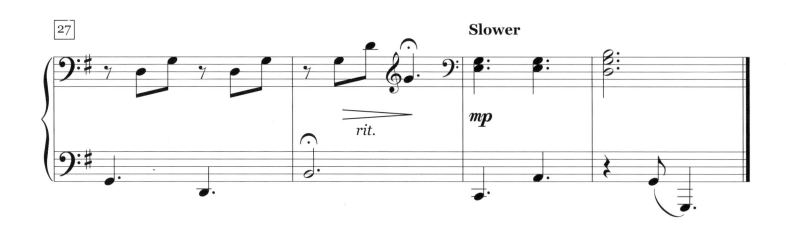

PRIMO

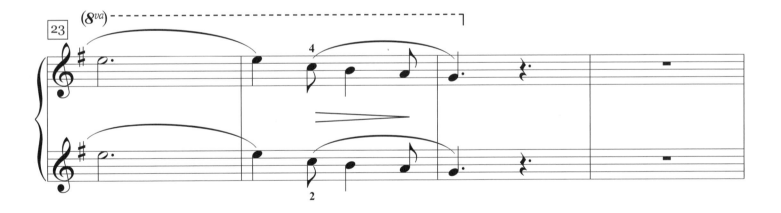

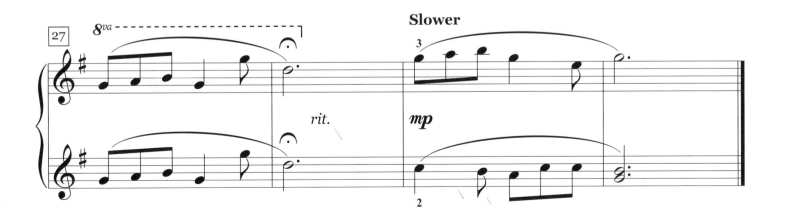

Symphonie Concertante
Op. 6, No. 1, 1st mvmt.

SECONDO

Chevalier de Saint-Georges
1745–1799
Arranged by Eric Baumgartner

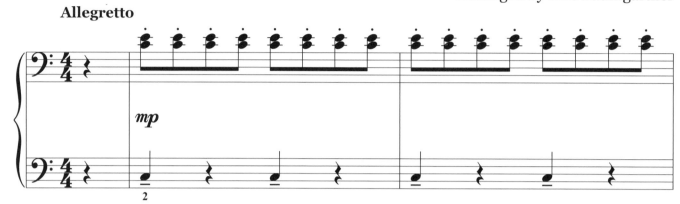

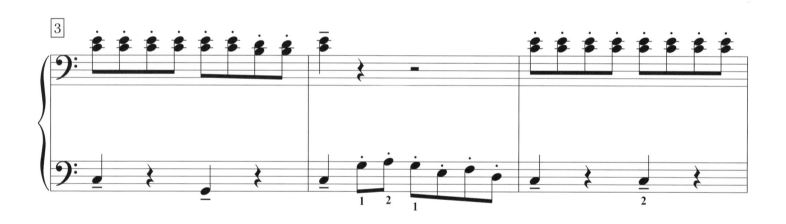

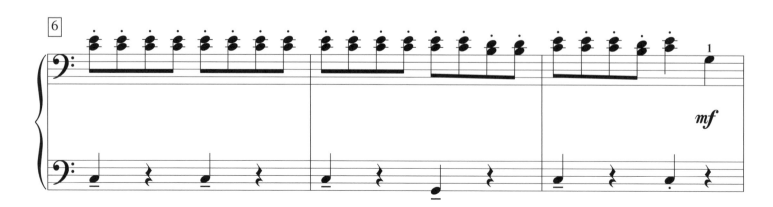

Symphonie Concertante
Op. 6, No. 1, 1st mvmt.

PRIMO

Chevalier de Saint-Georges
1745–1799
Arranged by Eric Baumgartner

SECONDO

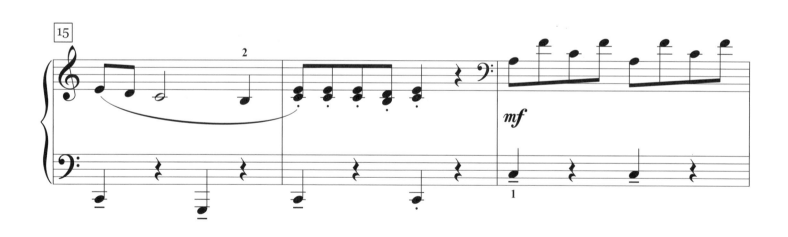

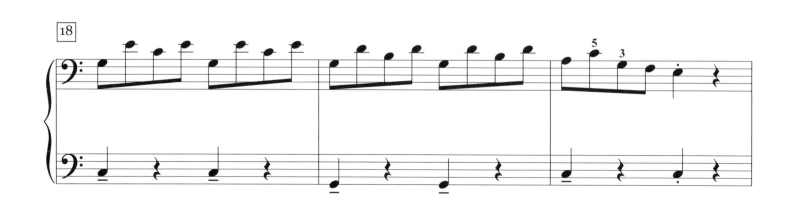

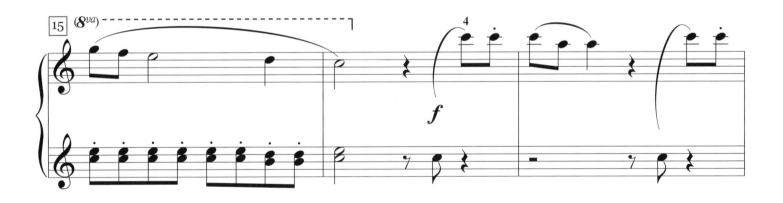

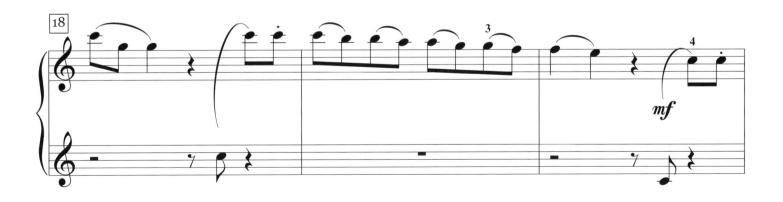

SECONDO

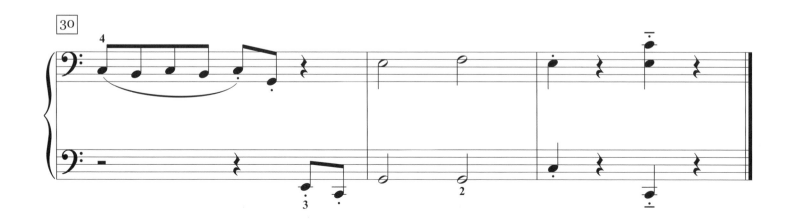

PRIMO

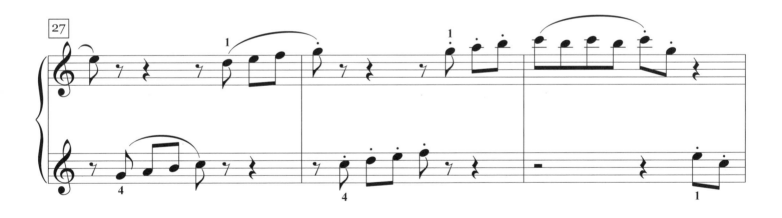

Flower Duet
from *Lakmé*

SECONDO

Léo Delibes
1836–1891
Arranged by Glenda Austin

Sweetly flowing

Lightly pedal throughout

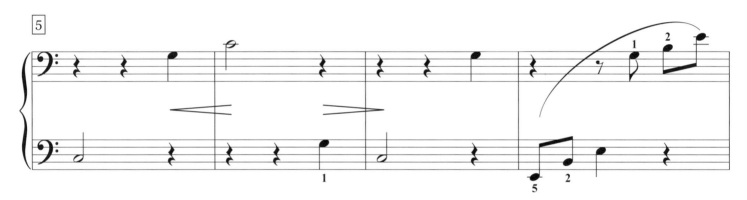

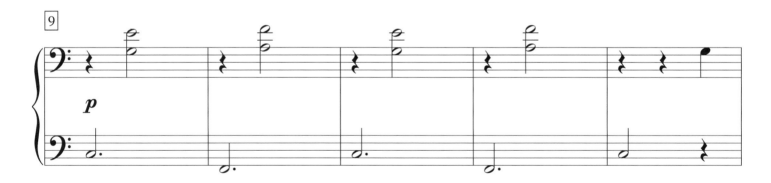

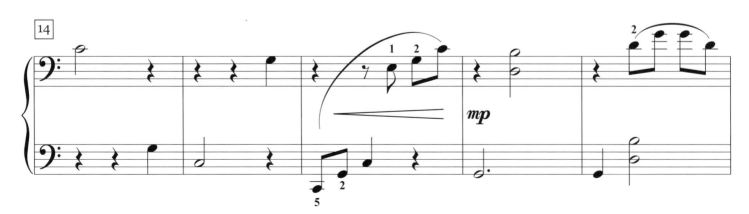

Flower Duet

from *Lakmé*

PRIMO

Léo Delibes
1836–1891
Arranged by Glenda Austin

Sweetly flowing

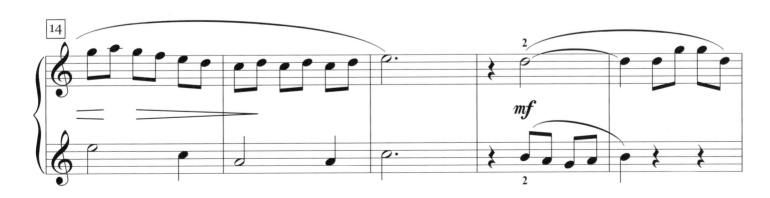

SECONDO

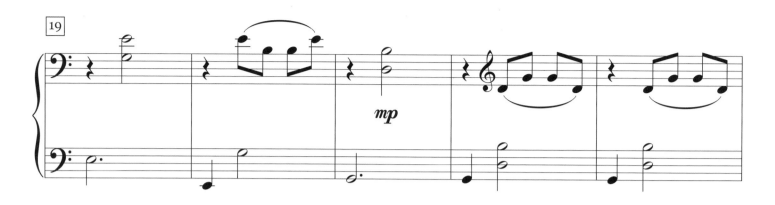

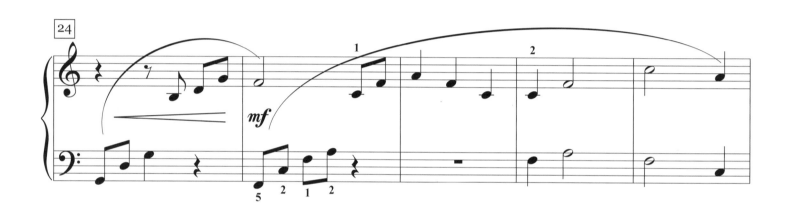

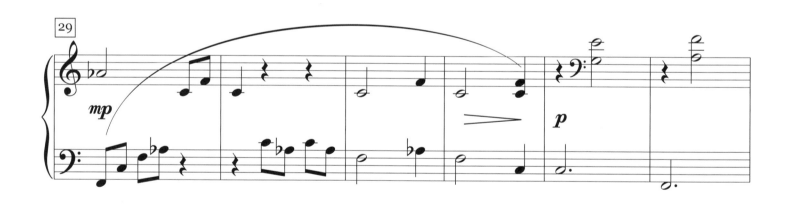

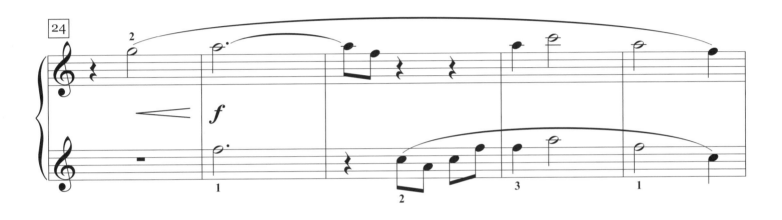

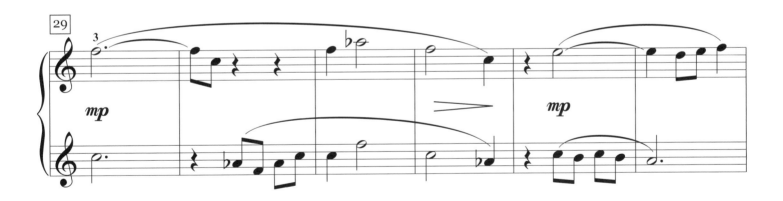

Jesu, Joy of Man's Desiring

SECONDO

Johann Sebastian Bach
1685–1750
Arranged by Carolyn Miller

Jesu, Joy of Man's Desiring

PRIMO

Johann Sebastian Bach
1685–1750
Arranged by Carolyn Miller

Moderato

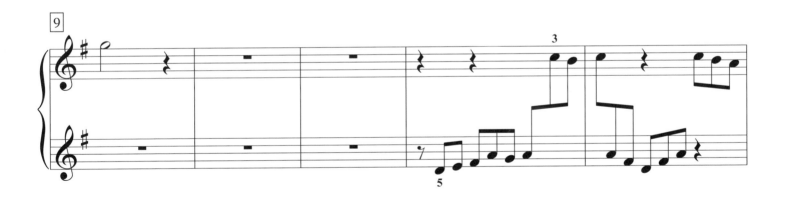

SECONDO

SECONDO

PRIMO

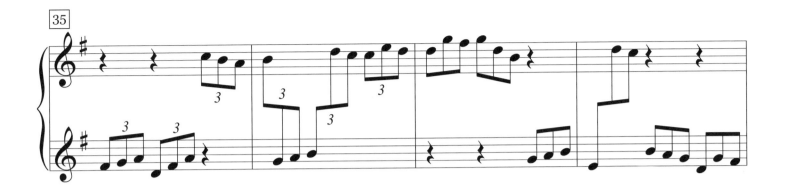

Canon in D

SECONDO

Johann Pachelbel
1653–1706
Arranged by Melody Bober

Canon in D

PRIMO

Johann Pachelbel
1653–1706
Arranged by Melody Bober

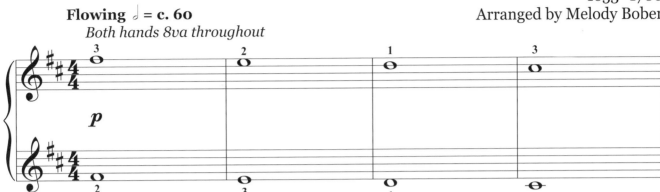

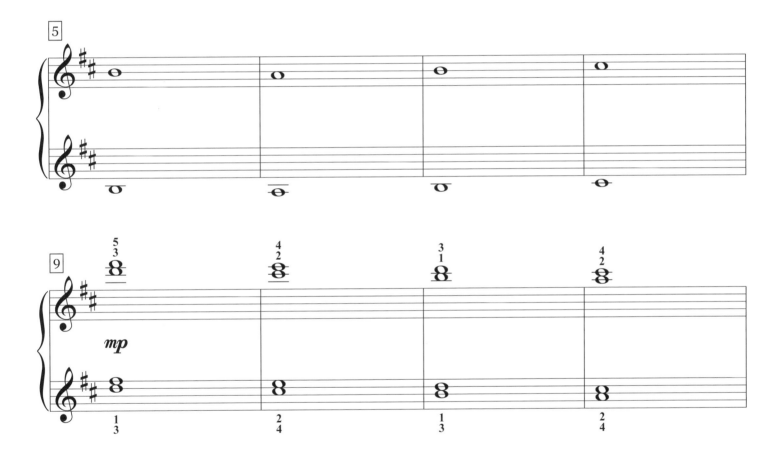

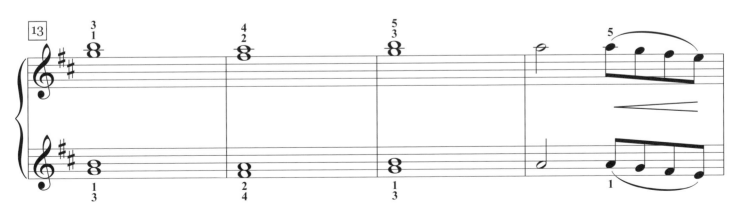

SECONDO

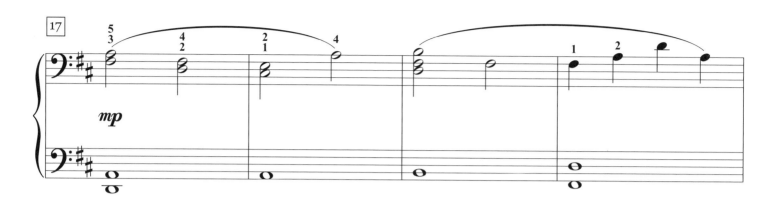

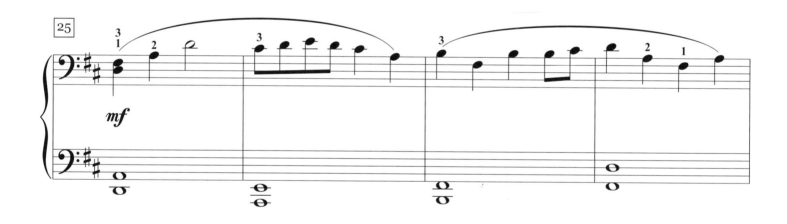

PRIMO

SECONDO

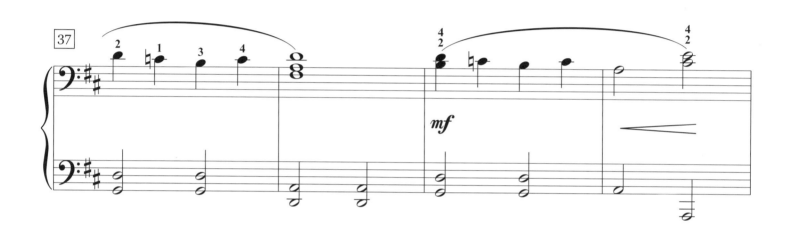

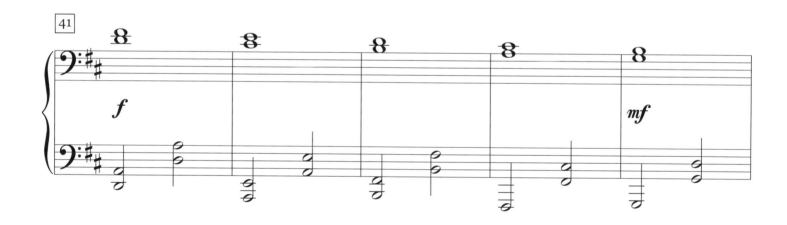

PRIMO

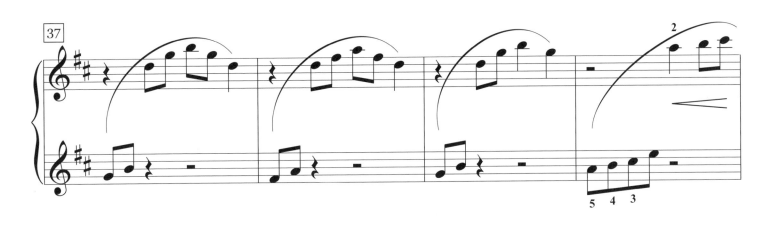

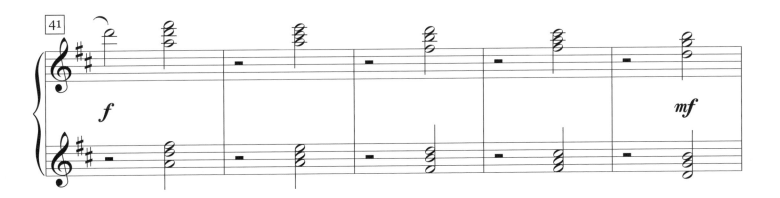

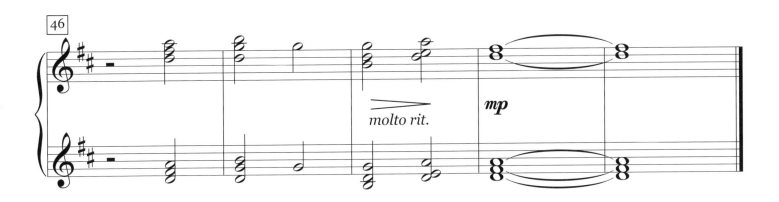

Vocalise
Op. 34, No. 14

SECONDO

Sergei Rachmaninoff
1873–1943
Arranged by Eric Baumgartner

Molto cantabile

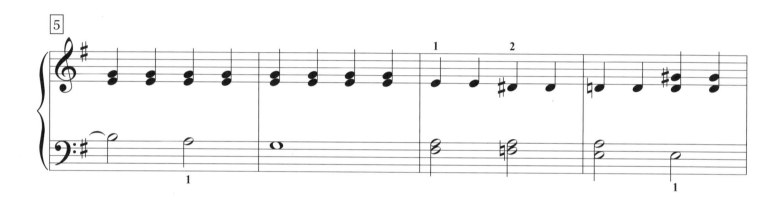

With light pedal (sempre legato)

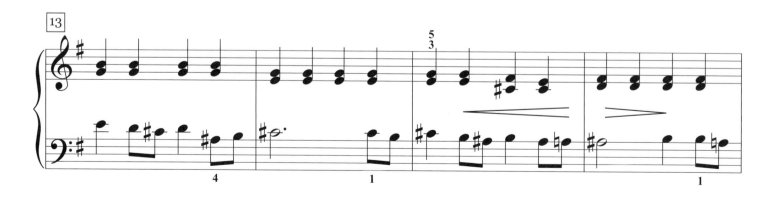

Vocalise
Op. 34, No. 14

PRIMO

Sergei Rachmaninoff
1873–1943
Arranged by Eric Baumgartner

Molto cantabile

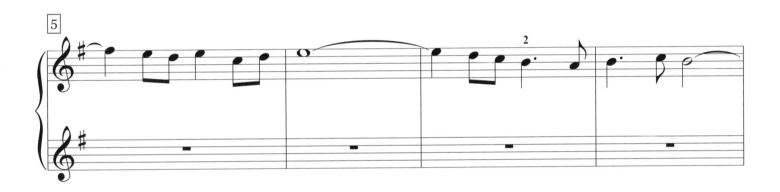

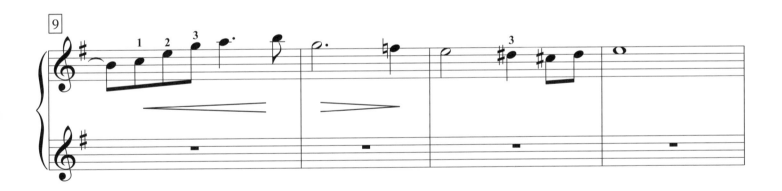

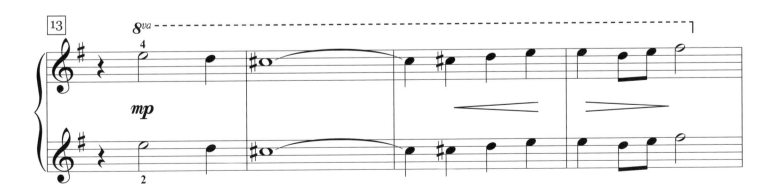

SECONDO

PRIMO

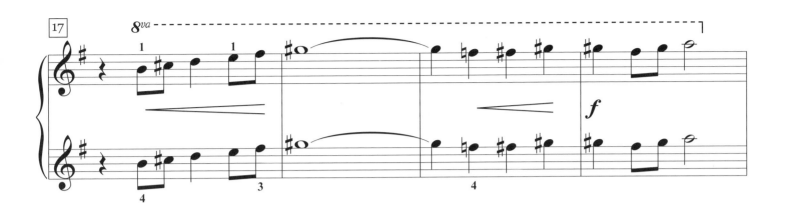

Piano Trio in G Minor
Op. 17, 1st mvmt.

SECONDO

Clara Schumann
1819–1896
Arranged by Melody Bober

Piano Trio in G Minor
Op. 17, 1st mvmt.

PRIMO

Clara Schumann
1819–1896
Arranged by Melody Bober

SECONDO

PRIMO

SECONDO

PRIMO

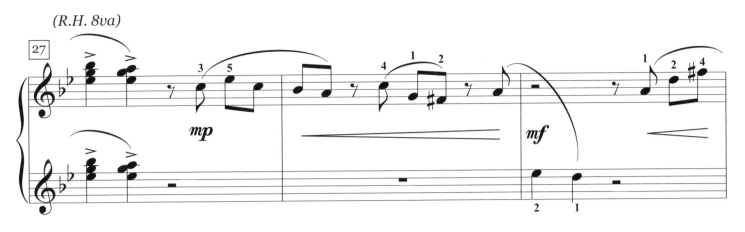

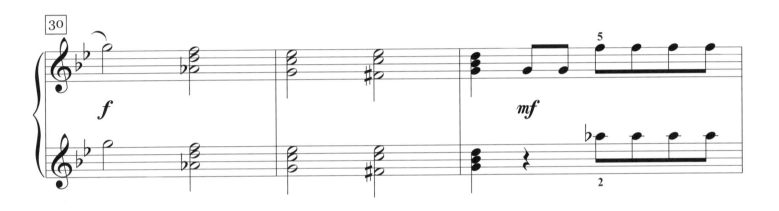

MORE DUET COLLECTIONS
FROM WILLIS MUSIC

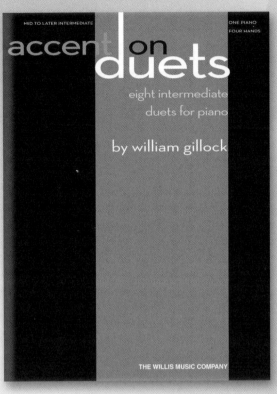

Glenda Austin is a pianist, arranger, and composer who writes piano music popular at all levels. She graduated from the University of Missouri (Columbia) with a bachelor's degree in music education and a master's degree in piano performance. Glenda has over 40 years' experience as an elementary and high school music teacher, and holds memberships in the Music Teachers National Association and Missouri Music Educators Association. A frequent adjudicator and clinician, she has presented workshops for teachers and students throughout the United States, as well as in Canada and Japan. In addition, she is collaborative pianist for the choral department at Missouri Southern State University. Married to high-school sweetheart, David, they are the parents of Susan and Scott, and grandparents of Isaac, Eden, and Levi.

Eric Baumgartner received jazz degrees from Berklee College of Music and DePaul University. He is the author and creator of Jazz Piano Basics, a series that presents jazz fundamentals in an accessible manner through short dynamic exercises. Eric is a sought-after clinician who has presented throughout the US, Canada, England, Germany, and Australia. He and his wife Aretta live in Atlanta, Georgia where he maintains an active schedule as performer, composer, and dedicated member of the local music scene.

Melody Bober enjoys creating motivational piano pieces that foster her students' understanding and love of music. She graduated summa cum laude from the University of Illinois at Champaign-Urbana with a bachelor's degree in music education. She later received a Master of Arts degree in piano performance from Minnesota State University, Moorhead. Melody credits much of her success to her influential teachers who include Joel Shapiro, Andrew Froelich, Mary Hoffman, and Tony Caramia. In addition to teaching piano in her private studio, Melody's music-teaching experience includes 20 years of public school and two years at the university level. A dynamic clinician and innovative composer, she is in demand at conventions and workshops for piano teachers across North America. She resides in Minnesota with her husband Jeff.

Carolyn Miller is a teacher, pianist, and composer from Cincinnati, Ohio. She holds music degrees from the College Conservatory of Music at the University of Cincinnati and Xavier University. She has taught piano to students of all ages for many years, both private and in the classroom, and often adjudicates at music festivals and competitions. Her music teaches essential technical skills, yet is fun to play, which appeals to both children and adults. Many of her compositions appear on contest lists, including the NFMC Festivals Bulletin. Carolyn also directs a large church choir and is the pianist for special services. She enjoys spending time with her husband Gary and their entire family, especially her seven grandchildren.